# Unlocking the Secrets of Body Language: How you can use it in your everyday life

I0417273

By Mr. Lee

# Table of Contents

# Chapter 1

## Back to basics: Why body language matters.

Beyond the words, beyond the sound of our voice, there is so much more to interpersonal communication than the words we choose or even the way in which we say them. Many studies have shown that when we are engaged in conversation only around thirty five percent of our communication is verbal whilst the majority of what we communicate is actually conveyed through an intricate combination of non-verbal signals and messages, otherwise known as body language. Furthermore, first impressions, formed within the first four to five minutes of meeting someone, are also largely based on non-verbal information. These valuable first impressions can count for up to ninety percent of what we think of that person as a whole! So, when we consider the question of whether body language matters, in terms of how it affects our communication skills and the success of our interpersonal relationships, the answer is a resounding yes. The secrets of body language that are revealed in the following chapters will demonstrate just how important an aspect of life our non-verbal communication is and how powerfully it can influence the way that we view, and are viewed, by others.

Despite what we may think about how open-minded we are or how cautious we should be in making snap judgments about people, we cannot completely avoid the subconscious assessments that occur when we meet people for the first time. Opinions about the person's attitude, approachability, status and attractiveness are formed through the powerful non-verbal messages of body language. Body language is absolutely central to how we navigate our interpersonal relationship and can even eliminate the need for words in certain situations. Certain body language signals transcend social and cultural differences and there are many studies that identify these non-verbal forms of communication as deeply rooted in our biology.

Once we know the incredible power that our body language holds in terms of how we communicate and interact with each other, it is absolutely astounding that so may of us are unaware of the postures, movements and gestures that we use every single day. Our body language holds the key to what we are really thinking and feeling, which may not always be the same as the words that are coming from our mouth. Understanding body language is a valuable tool that can be used in all aspects of our life and in all situations where we are interacting with other people. Most people will already possess an 'innate' or subconscious understanding of body language, but by bringing this understanding into the realms of conscious thought we can begin to tap into its real power.

The mind and the body are inextricably linked and each exerts a powerful force over the other.

When we accept this fact it is easy to understand how our thoughts influence our body language and conversely how our body language can affect the way that we feel. For example, if we are feeling nervous or lacking in confidence we might stand with our shoulders curled forward, hold our own arm for comfort and bend our head down slightly. This body language actually reinforces the emotions that are causing us to stand in this posture. To help us to combat these negative feelings of self-doubt we can consciously decide to alter our body language to stand up straighter, to push our shoulders back, release our arms and lift our head up. By doing this, the physical movements and posture of your body will instead create positive feelings of confidence which transmit all the way from your body to your mind.

Another wonderful example of the incredible effect that our body language can have on the way that we feel is laughter. Even if we force ourselves to laugh or we are laughing for no good reason, it will improve our mood. More amazingly still, scientific studies have shown that laughter can actually have a positive effect on our physical health and even be a positive tool in combatting disease. Smiling works in a similar way, releasing feel-good hormones into our system and improving our mood. Just the physical action of smiling has been proven to increase positive feelings even when the smile is not genuine! Of course this also means that body language can have a negative effect on how we feel, so being aware of what body language we are using can actually prevent us from making ourselves or others feel unnecessarily bad.

A common a mistake that someone beginning to learn about the secrets of body language will make is to look at a pose or a gesture in isolation from other signs and signals. Sometimes a person really does have an itch on their nose and it is not a sign that they are struggling to deceive you. Sometimes that person is sweating because they are hot or they just ran to catch the bus and not because they are incredibly nervous. Body language is a complex combination of gestures, movements and signals and it is the way in which they are used in conjunction with one another that will reveal the true message. The context of each individual situation is also incredibly important in deciphering the secret messages of body language, and cultural and social norms can also have a profound influence on the meanings attached to certain types of non-verbal communication.

When we describe someone as 'perceptive' or 'intuitive' we are actually noticing their ability to read non-verbal messages. Some people are much better than others at subconsciously interpreting body language and analyzing it in terms of how it corresponds with the verbal messages that the other person is conveying. It is this skill in the evaluation and interpretation of body language that allows some people to have what may seem to be a 'magical' or unexplained ability to read people or to describe a situation with uncanny precision. The good news for those of us who don't already possess such skills is that they can be learnt and that with improved awareness and understanding we can quickly begin to see the positive effects of uncovering the secrets of body language.

# Chapter 2

## Read my lips: Are smiles and laughter always what they seem?

A smile can speak a thousand words, overcome language barriers, and is a powerful initial way of expressing goodwill and our general openness to further interaction. Smiling is a universally accepted gesture that is usually submissive in nature and is mostly used to express positive feelings such as happiness, enjoyment and amusement.  However, not all smiles are quite what they seem and most of us are more than familiar with situations where we find ourselves faking a smile whether it be for a posed photograph, meeting an ex-partner's new spouse or agreeing to a request from your new boss.

When we dig a little deeper into the secrets behind the smile we discover that there are many types of smiles, both genuine and fake, and that they can reveal a much bigger story than simply being happy.

The ability to recognize different types of smiles is a deeply ingrained part of our body language. For our ancient ancestors, successfully recognizing what is a genuinely submissive smile as opposed to an aggressive grimace may have been key to their survival as they faced situations where distinguishing friend from foe was a case of life or death. Whilst the need for recognizing different types of smiles may be less dramatic in our modern lives today, there are still a lot of benefits to be gained from the insights that a deeper understanding of these subtle signals may bring.

Here are just a few of the different types of smile that we tend to encounter in everyday life and how to tell them apart.

- **The 'hello I'm friendly' smile:** The face will be relaxed and the corners of the mouth pull upward. Depending on how much emotion is behind the smile it may or may not extend upwards to affect the area around the eyes. This kind of smile may be an automatic reaction to a smile from another and is used as an icebreaker to signal that the person has friendly intentions towards you. This is the smile most often used when meeting new people, so although it may not always be the most genuine, it does tend to reveal an honest openness towards others.

- **The 'real deal' smile:** This is the smile that is most difficult to fake as it extends to many parts of the face including an open mouth, teeth shown, and a relaxed 'smiling' gaze. The easiest way to be sure that this kind of smile is genuine to look at the eyes. The small wrinkles that become visible at the side of the eyes are an automatic response to genuine amusement or pleasure and very hard to fake convincingly.

- **The 'keeping quiet' smile:** The mouth remains closed and the lips are often pursed or stretched tightly. The smile may give a straight line across or just a slight upward curve. This smile can be a sign that the person is keeping something from you. Look to the person's eyes for a better indication of what they are really thinking if they are presenting you with this type of smile.

- **The 'oh how nice' smile:** A subtle variation on the 'keeping quiet' smile, this smile is used to appear polite. The lips are held tightly in a slight upward curve but often the rest of the face will be tell a different story with a slight frown to the eye and forehead areas. It may be used in situations when the person is unsure of the situation, or when they are trying to hide another less positive emotion.

- **The 'come along now' smile:** This smile is most often seen when someone is trying to persuade or coerce you into something. The person may be tipping their head down and slightly to one side as they look up at you. A telltale sign of this smile is that there may be a hint of a frown in their face as their inner eyebrows move slightly upwards to express a request.

- **The 'bee to a honey pot' smile:** With similarities to the 'come on now' smile, this is smile where you will notice the head is turned down and slightly away while the person is looking up. Usually the smile will be with fairly tight lips and either a closed or very a slightly open mouth. This smile conveys a youthful, mischievous spirit as well as a sense of playful secrecy. People often use this type of smile to endear themselves to the others and, when used well, it can be very effective in winning a person's affection or perhaps even seducing them.

- **The 'trying too hard' smile:** Recognizable by the fact that despite the smile being a fairly broad smile that extends across the sides of the face only the top row of teeth are visible and the eyes are not engaged in the expression. This smile can mean that the person has a hidden agenda or is being insincere.

- **The 'think again' smile:** If you look closely at this type of smile you can see almost opposite emotions on the two sides of the face. One half of the face displays a smile often coupled with a widened eye and raised eyebrow. On the other side of the face the mouth is neutral and the eye area may display a doubtful or angry frown. This expression usually reveals sarcasm or conflicting emotions. If you recognize this expression in a person you would be wise to think carefully before taking their words or actions at face value.

Smiling is remarkably contagious and amazingly the smile does not need to be sincere for our subconscious mind to mirror what we see. Of course we can consciously overrule this natural reaction, but more often than not we will imitate the expressions we see even when we might be trying not to. Studies have shown that it is especially difficult to respond to a positive facial expression with a negative, for example meeting a smile with a frown. We automatically want to respond by copying the expressions that we see and therefore connect with the messages we are receiving from the other person. In terms of body language, smiling is an incredibly important part of how other people respond to you. Being able to smile and respond to a smile, even if it is not completely heartfelt, produces positive reactions in others.

Smiling is not just good for the soul it also makes good business sense. Various studies have shown that smiling at a pertinent time such as the beginning of a negotiation or when you first meet a new business associate creates a positive response in both parties which leads to a higher rate of success for all involved. Some people find it easy to smile and may be described as having a 'sunny' disposition. Conversely, there are some people who seem to rarely crack a smile. Of course there can be many different reasons why people don't smile, our first assumption will most likely be that they are simply not happy and whilst this may be correct in some cases we may also be wise to dig a little deeper into the reasons that they maintain a more serious facial expression.

Various studies reveal that people who rarely smile are often those who are in a position of dominance, or who wish to be viewed as dominant. Whilst smiling signals to the other person that you are non-threatening, not smiling is a way to avoid appearing submissive. There are many powerful individuals who we will rarely see smiling, a clever way for them to assert their dominance and portray a superior or aggressive attitude towards others. When these people do smile it will often be with tight lips and a purposeful message of a lack of willingness to reveal themselves and their real emotions. Research shows that there is also a difference between the sexes in terms how people respond to a lack of smiling. Men who don't smile tend to be viewed as expressing strength and dominance while women who don't smile are often viewed as expressing displeasure or anger. Perhaps as a result of this the average woman actually smiles considerably more than her male counterpart and is more likely to smile even when it does not reflect her true feelings. For this reason it may be more difficult to distinguish between the practiced smiles of a female than a male when trying to decipher the hidden secrets behind the smile.

Similar to smiling, when laughter is part of how we interact with people in our everyday it has a plethora of positive effects. Laughing helps us to make friends, to appear attractive and even to maintain better health. Our whole body benefits when we laugh as it improves circulation, lowers the heart rate and even burns calories. Laughter is a powerful tool against depression and many studies have proved that what some people term 'laughter therapy' can even have a significant effect in curing other illnesses. With this type of therapy the laughter does not even have to be real, the effects of laughing appear to be very similar whether the laughter is sincere or not. One possible explanation for this is that laughter, similar again to smiling, can actually create the feelings of happiness associated with the action even if the real feelings are initially absent. An example of this is a 'laughing circle' where a group of people lies down with their heads touching and one person starts laughing and people join in until everyone is laughing together. The laughter may be forced at first but eventually the laughter becomes very real.

One reason that we are attracted to people who smile and laugh is because by being around them we will tend to mirror them and therefore smile and laugh more ourselves. When we are smiling and laughing regularly we will not only feel the benefits in terms of our mood but also our health and general well being. Conversely, if we often find ourselves in the company of people who don't smile or laugh we are likely to mirror their expressions and feel less happy and perhaps even become ill.

As with smiling, there are many different types of laugh and often people will laugh in different ways at different occasions. By identifying different laughs we can gain more valuable insight into the person's emotions and personality. Here are a few of the most common types of laugh we are likely to encounter and what they reveal.

- **The 'louder than life' 'laugh:** This laugh is highly contagious and will often inspire people to join in, though they may be laughing at the laugh as opposed to the original joke. Expressive and genuine in nature, this type of laugh usually indicates that the person is fun, outgoing and sincere.

- **The 'performance' laugh:** Although the right kind of sounds may be being produced, there is something not quite right about this laugh and closer inspection will show that the upper parts of the face are unaffected. People laughing in this way are usually seeking attention or trying quite hard to make a certain impression whilst maintaining control over their real emotions.

- **The 'cry and giggle' laugh:** This laugh leaves you feeling unsure about whether the person is actually laughing or crying. The sound comes out in short bursts and the mouth may be fairly neutral or even turned slightly down at the edges in an unhappy expression. We will usually hear this laugh when someone is nervous or feeling guilty about something.

- **The 'child-like' laugh:** Starting with a natural, impulsive burst of laughter or giggling, the person will often then put their hand to their mouth in a cutesy 'oops' kind of gesture. This type of display is attention seeking and the person using it is looking to endear themselves to others around them or seeking some type of reassurance. It can also be a way of encouraging other people to share their child-like 'naughtiness' or amusement.

- **The 'trying not to' laugh:** The type of laugh that emerges when we are not entirely sure we should be laughing. It comes in many styles, some of which are almost silent and involve the body convulsing while very little noise is made. In others the laugh comes out in short, stifled bursts and again is usually accompanied by tell tale body movements such as putting the hand to the mouth, shoulders shaking and body curling over. There are many reasons that people laugh in this way, including shyness or guilt for finding something amusing in the first place. The funny thing about this type of laugh is that we will often find that the more we try to stop ourselves from laughing, the more intense it can actually become. This laugh can be very contagious and it may be very difficult to stop yourself from joining in when you see someone displaying this type of laugh.

- **The 'bashful chuckle':** A loud continuous chuckle accompanied by slightly bashful body language such as hands touching the face and body pulled inwards, this shows that a person is spontaneous yet self-aware. The laugh will tend to be very genuine as this is a difficult combination to fake.

- **The 'girly giggle' laugh:** Usually seen in people who wish to appear sweet and harmless, whether male or female, this laugh signifies that the person is happy to be part of whatever fun is going on at the time. The quieter the giggle, the more likely it is that the person is shy or lacking in self-confidence and is seeking reassurance from others around them. Louder giggles tend to be a response to contagious laughter and a display of empathy and enjoyment. Giggles are one of the most likely types of laugh for people to fake, but it is often easy to spot as real giggling engages the face and eyes whilst fake displays will be much more about the noise produced.

# Chapter 3

## The eyes are portals to our souls: How to see people for who they really are.

Eye contact is an essential part of human interaction and gives us important information about how to proceed during a conversation, how the other person is feeling and whether or not they are being truthful with us. When face-to-face with another person we will tend to spend the majority of the time looking at their eyes and mouth to understand what they thinking. The non-verbal language that our eyes convey is possibly the most reliable source of information we can gain from understanding body language. It can also be the most difficult to pay attention to as the movements are subtle and happen quickly. The direction that our eyes move in, the type of gaze and even the size of our pupils can reveal a lot about how we are feeling or what we are thinking as we interact with others.

A simple example that most people will quickly be able to recognize is the overall eye contact of someone who is listening to you talk. If the person is looking straight ahead or directly at you, it means that they are simply receiving your information. If the person is looking downwards it means that they are assessing what you are saying. Looking past you or eyes focused on something else is an indication that they are distracted or disinterested and if the person avoids eye contact entirely it is a good indication that they are feeling very nervous or unsure of the entire situation.

Another aspect of eye contact that we can learn about is the 'gaze' or the way that we look at someone. The type of gaze that we use in different situations is important in terms of social interactions and what is an appropriate type of gaze in one situation may be completely disastrous in another. It is easy to recognize that the way we might gaze lovingly into the eyes of our partner or child will not be so well received by a business associate or the cashier in a shop. So what are the main types of gaze that we switch so intuitively between in our everyday lives and how are they different?

- **The 'friends and social situations' gaze:** A friendly gaze where the eyes look from the eyes to the mouth as well as brief looks towards the rest of the body or the general surroundings. This gaze is short and will last a maximum of two to three seconds with eyes travelling to look at various features of the face, hair and body. When direct eye contact is made with the other person it will be held fairly briefly before one or both parties look away.

- **The 'romantic' gaze:** When two people are attracted to each other they will engage in a series of eye movements and interactions. Usually there will be some an intense initial gaze where both people hold direct eye contact before looking away. The 'romantic' gaze is characterized by the fact that it lasts longer than a 'friendly sociable' gaze and in some cases can comfortably be held for up to four or five seconds. After this initial show of interest the eyes may then move to examine the rest of the face more closely, though the eyes and mouth will remain the focuses of the overall gaze. Glances away will be to note other physical features of the person including their body and what they are wearing.

- **The 'professional' gaze:** This type of gaze varies considerably depending on who you are talking to and the power play between you. It can be difficult to discern the exact amount of time that it is appropriate to hold a 'professional' gaze for and we will usually depend on cues from the other person to decide this in each specific situation. Generally women are comfortable with holding eye contact for longer with each other whilst if a male counterpart holds a gaze for too long the woman may start to feel uncomfortable. Holding a gaze for too long between two men can be a sign of aggression or a struggle for dominance of the situation. In professional situations we should avoid allowing our gaze to fall below the shoulders so as to clearly give a message that our focus is on business and not romantic or sexual in any way. In this way our 'professional' gaze can still give a message of genuine interest and intention without those intentions being misinterpreted.

In a typical 'professional' gaze here are some tips to help you assess the attitude that the other person is taking towards you.

- **The eyes are focused on you or straight ahead:** They are passively receiving information and are listening carefully.

- **They hold constant eye contact:** They are being aggressive or getting ready to challenge you in some way.

- **The eyes move to the right hand side as they break eye contact:** They are actively thinking about what you are saying.

- **The eyes move to the left hand side as they break eye contact:** They are relating what you are saying to a past experience or to some other information.

- **The eyes move downward as they break eye contact:** They are drawing on something emotional or complex in considering your words.

- **Looking away from you or focusing on other things in the room:** They are not entirely focused or interested in what you are saying. This can also be a sign that they are waiting for the conversation to come to an end.

- **The eyes regularly look upwards:** They are engaged in careful analytical thought and relating your words to their own thoughts and feelings.

Other than responding to lightness and darkness, our pupils also change size depending on how we are feeling. Our pupils will become larger, or dilate, when we are stimulated or excited by something and will become smaller, or contract, when we see something that we don't like. Studies have shown that we will view the same person as more attractive when their pupils are dilated because we are subconsciously picking up on the fact that they are feeling positive or stimulated. When we are attracted to someone our eyes will tend to give us away as our pupils will dilate and our eyes will open. These signals are usually understood subconsciously and we are naturally drawn to larger pupils in all types of situations. Children and infants have larger pupils than adults that serve appeal for attention and also gain reciprocal interest and positivity from people looking at them. Our pupils are another example of mirroring in body language, as when we look at someone whose pupils are dilated our pupils will usually dilate in response.

# Chapter 4

## Secret Sign Language: Revealing the truth behind hand gestures

Whilst hand gestures are usually used to enhance meaning and animate our conversations, it is said that the origin of the Italian hand gestures language was in fact to prevent conversations from being overheard and was a form of secret sign language. Italian hand gestures are so incredibly expressive and widely understood that they even have their own dictionary. Physiologically, our hands are one of the most important things that separate us from other animal species and we have more neural connections linking our brain to our hands than any other part of our body. Despite this, most of us will pay little attention to the 'talking' that our hands do without us even thinking about them.

Showing or hiding our hands can give important non-verbal messages and strong indications about our attitude towards others. Our hands are an important way that we express whether or not we are honest and non-threatening. Our ancestors would have used open hands to show that they were not concealing weapons and we continue to see this today when police officers demand to see 'hands in the air' or when we show open hands with palms up to express that we don't have or don't know something. Even when we wave to say 'hello' or hold a hand up, palm forward, to say 'hi' we are actually practicing this age-old display of having nothing to hide. Conversely, hiding our hands will send the opposite message and may make other people feel wary or suspicious of us. Think of a lawyer patrolling the courtroom with their hands behind their back. This gives the impression that they are withholding something from us, that they still have 'ammunition' that we are currently unaware of. Concealing our hands or can be a way of asserting power or dominance over others and can be used to our advantage in situations where we want to appear confident and in control.

Watching the way someone moves or displays their hands is also one of the best ways to judge their honesty. When someone is being genuine and telling the truth, they will subconsciously use hand gestures that show the palms of their hands, which we will in turn experience as a non-verbal message of honesty and trustworthiness. Showing the palms of our hands is an open hand gesture and shows an attitude of honesty, openness and submission, while concealing our palms is a closed gesture that can signify anxiety, aggression or dominance. A hand gesture that most people will be very familiar with is that of someone's hands clenched into fists, a clear sign of anger or frustration. The stronger the negative emotions, the tighter clenched the person's hands will be. Highly anxious emotions will also cause us to clench our hands or hold objects more tightly than usual. Another common hand gesture to take note of is when people place their hands in their pockets. This will tend to be a sign that the other person does not want to communicate with us.

Our hands may give us away when we are feeling anxious or stressed and many people will experience some degree of uncontrolled shaking in highly stressful situations. A tremble or shake in the hands can be caused by nervous excitement as well as pure fear and is a response that is very difficult to control, making it a form of non-verbal language that people will often try to disguise. To hide our shaking hands we might hold objects, grasp our hands together or maybe even keep our hands entirely out of the other person's sight. Looking at someone's hands can be an excellent indication of how relaxed or anxious they are really feeling as it is very difficult to keep your hands relaxed and in an open posture if you are actually highly stressed.

At the business table, hand signals are used to strengthen our verbal message. When we are appealing for something we will show open hands and upturned palms, whilst placing our hands face down in front of us demonstrates decisiveness, certainty and confidence. Salesmen are often trained to notice whether or not a client is displaying open palms when they are giving reasons why they are not willing to buy the product or enter into a business transaction. If the client is being truthful about why they aren't going to do business they will expose their palms, whilst if they are hiding something or telling a lie they will tend to hide the palms of their hands in some way. This knowledge can provide a valuable way of knowing when to continue with a sales pitch or to stop and avoid wasting time and energy on a lost cause.

The type of hand gesture that is most likely to provoke a negative response in others is finger pointing and is universally regarded as aggressive and rude. Studies show that when someone points their finger at us we actually listen less to what they are saying and instead adopt a defensive attitude and form negative judgments about whoever is pointing the finger. In order to make a point in an assertive way we can make a simple alteration to the straight finger point by opening the palm of the hand and bringing the finger to meet the thumb.

Responses to this type of gesture are much more positive and send listeners strong non-verbal signals of confidence, motivation and authority.

The handshake is another hand gesture that has become increasingly prominent in all circles of life and is now common in many more situations than its more traditional use in male-dominated business contexts. Despite this, there are still certain times that it may be inappropriate to greet someone with a handshake and we will generally need to take our cue from the other person and the context in which we are meeting. If we initiate a handshake with someone who does not want to shake our hand it will generally cause an uncomfortable atmosphere and in some cases may make the person withdraw from the situation entirely. On the other hand, a good friendly handshake can be an excellent icebreaker when meeting someone for the first time and allows a brief, safe form of contact and welcome. Shaking hands also allows us to briefly enter the other's personal space and make closer eye contact, creating an opportunity to connect through a variety of non-verbal cues.

How we shake hands gives powerful subliminal messages to the people we meet and although most people can remember a particularly bad type of handshake we actually don't tend to consciously register the subtleties of the message conveyed by a regular handshake. Broadly speaking, we will subconsciously register one of three things when we shake hands with someone, either that they are equal to us, weaker than us or stronger than us. Even if we lack a conscious recognition of the message received by a handshake it can still have a significant effect on the outcome of further interactions with that person. For example, if the person's handshake conveys a message of being weaker than us we might view them as easy to dominate, which will in turn effect the way that we approach our dealings with them. If our aim is to make that person feel comfortable or enter into a relationship of trust and equality we may adjust our attitude to be less threatening. Conversely, if our aim is for them to submit to our demands or enter into a relationship where we are in control we may draw on and enhance our position of power.

There are some types of handshake that are almost universally disliked and that we should avoid giving in normal circumstances. Of course, when operating in international spheres there are cultural differences that we would be wise to be aware of such as the soft handshake that is preferred in some Asian countries. As a general rule of thumb though, certain handshakes will receive a negative response and should be used with extreme caution.

Here is a quick guide to some of the most common handshakes and what they reveal about the person.

- **The 'dead fish' handshake:** The extended hand is limp and there is no grasping motion from the hand or fingers. The physical softness of the hand also translates into a view of the person as without real form or strength. People who use this type of handshake are giving the impression that they are weak and unresponsive. This handshake may also be used by people, especially women, who wish to remain delicate, elusive or disinterested in the eyes others.

- **The 'over-enthusiastic' handshake:** The main characteristic of this handshake is a firm grasp combined with a lot of arm movement. Whilst a regular handshake should last around three seconds and involve the hands moving up and down between three to six times, this handshake will engage the arms more vigorously to move the whole of arms and sometimes even knock someone off their balance! The 'over-enthusiastic' hand (and arm!) shake can last more than six seconds and signals an energetic and perhaps over-bearing person who wants to be involved.

- **The 'finger grab' handshake:** The strength of this handshake will focus on the fingers rather than the whole hand. This type of handshake conveys the message that the person would rather keep you at a distance. If they also squeeze your fingers hard it is probably a signal that they are trying to assert power over you and perhaps prevent you from challenging them.

- **The 'bone crusher' handshake:** The strength of the grip of this handshake may be so great that it is physically uncomfortable or even painful. The message behind this handshake is clear, this person wants you to know that they are powerful and a force to be reckoned with. In most situations you would be well advised to respond by keeping your composure and appearing confident. Don't enter into any kind of physical power struggle over the handshake because even if you 'win' the handshake, you will be losing face.

- **The 'trickster' handshake:** Beginning with a regular handshake the person then uses their other hand to either clasp the handshake or to grasp your shoulder or forearm. The genuine form of this handshake is reserved for close friends and for expressing warm and intimate feelings, so should be received with extreme caution from people other than those closest to you. People mostly use this type of handshake to fake a deeper connection, to gain trust that they will then use for their own gain. Be wary of people who use this type of handshake when it is clearly inappropriate, they are likely to have ulterior motives and are probably not very trustworthy.

- **The 'push away' handshake:** As the hand is released from the handshake there is a slight push away from one person. The proceeding handshake is usually brief and the message is that the person wants to keep you at a distance or may even be rejecting you in some way. This handshake can be way of conveying a warning and the firmer the push the more resolute the person is in informing you that you should 'back off'.

- **The 'pull in' handshake:** This handshake is another type of power play, as the person pulls you closer towards them and into their personal space. The most common reason that this handshake is used is to assert control or dominance over the other person. It can be a good indicator that the person will demand that you follow their lead or that they are may be likely to manipulate you in order to get what they want.

Being aware of the handshake technique that others are using can be a useful way to gain greater insight into the personality or attitude of a new acquaintance. Furthermore, with this insight you are also given an advantage in terms of how to proceed with the new relationship. It may seem hard to believe, but research suggests that up to ninety percent of what we think about someone is established within the first ninety seconds of meeting, making the handshake an important opportunity to make a positive first impression.

Having an appropriate handshake can considerably influence any face-to-face meeting, and it is possible to train yourself in the 'art of handshaking' to improve your prowess in this area. For example, in situations where we want to appear dominant we can consciously decide to use a 'palm down' handshake, where our hand is, to some degree, the upper hand in the handshake. On the other hand, we might want to give a feeling of power to the other person and therefore decide to use a 'palms up' handshake.

In most cases, a handshake is a way to build rapport and to convey some degree of friendliness. There are certain key factors that we can consider when ensuring the best chance of success with this kind of handshake. The first is to ensure that neither person has a noticeably 'upper palm' or 'lower palm' hand position. The two people's hands should be close to vertical. Secondly, the whole hand should be engaged in the handshake with fingers and palms grasping each other. Finally, the amount of pressure applied by each person should be close to equal as possible. There may be an instance, perhaps just a split second, of adjustment as both parties release or tighten the amount of pressure applied

so that the pressure exerted by each person is

equal.

# Chapter 5

## Below the belt: How legs and feet reveal our innermost thoughts

The legs and feet are an excellent way to unlock the secrets of our true intentions and wishes. They can also be the culprits for giving away our feelings about what we really want but haven't had the opportunity to do yet. We are all familiar now with how our hands and eyes can direct important non-verbal messages to the receiver, but not many people are aware that the feet also act in this way. In fact, whilst the average person may have some insight into how to read the body language of eyes and hands few will be well versed in the signals that feet convey. For this reason, noticing the placement of someone's feet is a great way to understand what his or her true intentions towards you are.

As a general rule, our feet will tend to point to where we want to be or where our attention is being held. If we are immersed in a conversation with someone and we are directing all our attention towards that person then our feet will be pointing towards them. Equally if we are trying to get someone's attention or we have strong positive feelings for that person our feet will again be clearly pointing in their direction. In another situation, we may be engaged in conversation with someone but our thoughts are really elsewhere or we are not feeling fully committed to the interaction in some way. In these instances our feet will be placed in a different direction, even if the rest of our body is turned towards them. If you notice that a person's feet are directed towards the door or the exit it may be a good signal that they actually want to leave. We might see feet pointed in this manner in stressful or unpleasant interactions.

Movement in the legs and feet can also be a signal that the person is eager to leave or is distracted in some way. Fidgeting with the feet due to boredom or a lack of interest will usually be accompanied by other non-verbal signals such as a mobile gaze, excessive hand movements and a general sense of restlessness. We will also find that our feet may become active when we are stressed or nervous, especially if we are making an effort to control other body language in an attempt to conceal our discomfort. Placing our feet firmly on the floor in the direction of the person with whom we are communicating can be a simple and effective way of preventing our feet from revealing our true feelings in these types of situations. Sometimes our feet may move or even 'dance' when we are struggling to contain positive emotions and are a sure sign of really genuine excitement or happiness.

While seated some people may adopt a position where the feet are wide apart and attention is being drawn to the crotch area. This is not necessarily a sexual display, but is mostly used to convey a message of confidence and relaxation. Depending on the situation it can also be an attempt to intimidate and can give the impression that you are in no way threatened by the other person. A seated position that relays a lack of confidence is sitting with your legs or ankles wrapped around the chair of the leg in a way that actually serves to restrict the movement of the legs. This type of position reveals a person who is struggling to keep something to themselves, or who is trying to contain some form of negativity. Both of these displays can be regarded as a basis for some suspicion as the over-confident 'crotch display' pose is often to convince you, or themselves, of how cool and relaxed they are while the seated chair leg wrap is a sign that the person is withholding something important and needs the physical presence of the chair to keep them in check.

When standing we can note several common ways that people stand and present their legs. Each pose suggests a different attitude or approach to the situation that they are encountering at that time. We will often shift between these different positions within the course of a conversation in response to the flow of events or interactions. Having an awareness of these different poses can allow us to understand and respond more effectively to other people and also give us the chance to practice and adapt our own body language for greater success in our social interactions.

- **The 'straight-up' stance:** When we stand with our legs straight and our feet fairly close together. This stance gives the

71

message that we are paying attention and that we are ready to engage. When we stand up straight in this pose it signifies respect and seriousness, such as a soldier standing to attention. A neutral amount of uprightness in the rest of the body displays honesty and a lack of concern over status. If the upper body is slouched whilst the legs and feet are straight the message is that of relaxation and a lack of formality, often seen between friends or close colleagues.

- **The 'strong man' stance:** Standing with our feet further apart than normal is a display of strength or power. The further apart the feet are, the more confidence the person is conveying with their legs. If the feet are shoulder-width apart in a stance it is a clear indicator that the person is 'ready for action' and feeling self-assured. By placing the hands on the hip area or leaning the upper body back slightly to further emphasize the crotch area, this pose can be made into a sexual display either to attract or to intimidate the other person.

- **The 'directing attention' stance:** If we stand with one foot slightly in front of the other, the direction that this first foot is pointing in shows the real direction of our attention. If we are interested in someone our foot will tend to naturally move or point in their direction and this is a subtle form of flirting that can be noticed when someone is shy or unsure of how the other person will respond to their advances. Similarly to the seated foot point, the forward foot when standing can also indicate that our focus is actually elsewhere or perhaps that we are waiting to leave the conversation altogether.

- **The 'ankle hug' stance:** The legs are close together and crossed or pressed tightly together at the ankle. This stance reveals that we are unsure or nervous about the situation and we are using this body language to subconsciously comfort and reassure ourselves. It is a submissive and protective posture and can also signify a difference in opinion or an overall resistance to open communication. We are most likely to find ourselves standing in this way when we meet someone for the first time and we feel shy or unsure of ourselves.

# Chapter 6

## If I said you had a beautiful body: Reading between the lines in dating and courtship

Research has shown that when a person encounters someone that they find attractive they will alter their body language to signal interest and to attract positive attention. Generally people respond by pushing their shoulders back, straightening their posture and walking with a new spring in their step. These changes serve to display a strong and youthful vitality and are often accompanied by other signs of either a dominant or submissive approach to a possible courtship. For example, a signals of dominance might be to tilt the head upwards to accentuate the chin whilst a submissive display may be to lower the chin and look up towards the other person. Body language is an essential aspect of courtship as it gives important signals about our interest, our availability and our desires. It is interesting to note that most of the body language we display when we are attracted to someone is natural and occurs subconsciously as opposed to being a practiced learnt behavior.

Surprisingly, the first signals sent in order to initiate a courtship are by the feminine or submissive person. The subtle body language involved in initial courtship type interactions are a complex combination of signals involving eye contact, leg and feet positions and hand gestures. These signals are perceived, often subconsciously, by the other person who may recall the subtle interactions as almost indescribable or simply that 'something about them caught my eye'. The chances of success for approaching a potential new partner increase significantly if they have first sent an invitation in the form of these subtle signals of interest. Whilst the submissive person will send the initial invitation, it is usually then up to the dominant person to continue the process. This means that, without a conscious recognition of the invitation signals being sent prior to what looks like the first real move, it will appear that the dominant person is initiating the courtship, as their response will be more noticeable. In this way the dominant party is able to feel in control and active in the interaction and the submissive party retains their coy and unassuming role.

A wide range of body language can be of the body can be interpreted as being sexual, such as crotch displays or an intense gaze, but they are only actually cues for courtship in the appropriate context. One such signal that can often be misread is accidental physical contact, such as brushing past someone in a small space. Many people can relate to this type of experience when you have completely innocently touched a stranger, perhaps on a busy train or when passing them in a store, and the person receiving this touch has turned to look at you in a suggestive way. Of course, in a different context and with intention this type of proximity and contact with someone can indeed signal sexual or romantic interest.

There are certain tactics that are often used by the submissive or feminine person in order to attract or hold the attention of someone they find attractive. Here is an easy to recognize list of some of the key signals that special someone is interested in you.

- **The 'delicate rose' signals:** The person will display delicate or vulnerable parts of the body such as the wrists and the neck. This serves to signal that although they are vulnerable they are willing to trust. Other signals of this type include making the body appear smaller by crossing the legs, pulling the shoulders together and forward and tilting the head.

- **The 'playful kitten' signals:** Coy smiles using a head tilt and an upward gaze to meet the other person's eyes are key to these courtship signals. A childlike mischievousness may also be conveyed by small but enthusiastic laughs and giggles, combined with wide eyes and a playful smile.

- **The 'sexy provocateur' signals:** Perhaps the most obvious indicators of sexual or romantic interest, these non-verbal signals enhance feminine features. Playing with hair, crossing the legs tightly and walking with a pronounced swing in the hips are some of the most common examples of this type of body language.

The clothes that we wear and how they reveal or accentuate parts of the body is also an example of provocative body language and serve to direct attention to the person's physical form.

- **The 'reducing personal space' signals:** As a courtship progresses from the first stolen glances to a romantic gaze and other indicators of attraction, the interested party will tend to reduce their amount of personal space and move closer to the other person. Extended eye contact and foot pointing may be used initially as they involve less risk of rejection. As we become more certain that the other person is interested this will tend to escalate to moving into closer proximity and some subtle physical contact such as touching their hand or arm as we speak to them.

Just as there are certain tactics used by the submissive or feminine person, we can also learn how to recognize the non-verbal signals that the more dominant or masculine person tend to use in courtship rituals. Here is a list of some of the most signals we might notice.

- **The 'healthy physique' signals:** Dominant people will seek to accentuate or draw attention to aspects of their physique that signal health, strength and virility. Postures that emphasize or increase the appearance of aspects such as broad shoulders, a flat stomach and overall muscularity are used to give signals that they are physically in good shape and able to provide for and protect a possible partner.

- **The 'sexual prowess' signals:**
  Postures that draw attention to the crotch area, such as sitting with legs wide apart, give signals that the person is sexual and masculine. Some of these signals may be subtle, such as placing hands on a belt or hooking fingers into belt loops, but serve the same purpose of drawing the eye to the crotch area. This type of body

language also displays confidence and sends messages that the person is successful and will be able to provide for their prospective partner.

- **The 'looking good' signals:** When people make small adjustments to their hair or clothes whilst in conversation they are actually sending non-verbal messages that they care about their appearance and are able to provide and care for themselves successfully. Beyond these adjustments, details of a person's overall appearance can also be key to transmitting 'looking good' signals and a prospective partner will consciously or subconsciously register aspects such as a clean and tidy appearance and add this to their impression of the person's character.

- **The 'calm and composed' signals:**
  The more dominant the person, the more likely they are to speak slowly in a calm and even tone. While the submissive person may be likely to chat away and become quite animated as they speak, the dominant party will tend to speak more concisely and with a sense of purpose. These signals again display a powerful sense of confidence, which can be very attractive in a partner.

- **The 'space invasion' signals:**
  Spreading the body to give the appearance

of being larger and to take up more space is a common signal seen in people displaying dominant body language. Postures and stances that expand the body send messages of strength, confidence and also make the person seem relaxed and at ease with the situation. This very open body language is a way of expressing that they are not feeling in the slightest bit threatened.

# Chapter 7

## Strike a pose: The body language of power plays and how to get ahead of the game

First impressions really do count and making a good first impression is one of the best ways to get ahead of the game in any situation. Body language really is key to a good first impression and research shows that up to ninety percent of what others think about you is formed within the first five minutes of meeting. Incredibly up to eighty percent of that opinion is formed from our non-verbal signals, making understanding these important secrets absolutely essential to our success in social interactions as a whole. Here are some top tips for using positive body language to create the best first impression possible, even in situations where you may be feeling anxious or stressed.

- **Walk with purpose:** Depending on the situation you will need to adjust the speed at which you walk. Walking slowly will make you appear casual and relaxed, which may be great for meeting new friends but not so appropriate for a job interview where it may be interpreted as a lack of motivation or interest. Walking too briskly may also give negative impressions of being hurried or overly anxious, so it is important to decide on the purpose of the meeting and walk with the appropriate speed and attitude.

- **Stand confidently:** Whatever the situation the most important of how you stand is to appear confident. Use open body language and beware of crossing your arms and legs, which immediately sends the message that you are holding back or feeling defensive. Instead, stand upright and try not to fidget with hands, arms, legs or feet. Your feet may be the most difficult part to keep in check, especially if you are feeling nervous, but by focusing on a good strong stance it is possible to prevent this telltale sign.

- **Sit upright and at a slight angle to the person:** A successful way to express interest and to show that you are ready to engage meaningfully with the other person is to retain good posture whilst seated. Slouching back in a chair will give the impression that you are not taking the meeting seriously or that you are not invested in the interaction. Try to keep a natural, relaxed but upright position and angle either your chair or your body slightly so as to avoid the fully face-on position that can be interpreted as confrontational.

- **Keep personal items organized:** Additional baggage or personal items can be an unwanted distraction or even give an impression of disorder, which can then reflect badly on you. By keeping your hands free where possible and personal items such as a bag, a folder or a coat organized and in check, the person will be more focused on you as opposed to whether or not you are about to drop something on the floor. Walking into an interview is a good example of when you would want to be able to place your personal items down easily and without fuss so that you can make eye contact and shake hands in a confident and timely manner.

- **A positive handshake:** An initial handshake should usually be fairly neutral in nature, not too dominant or submissive but with the aim of creating a sense of equality. To successfully shake hands in this way we should approach the person with our hand in a straight, vertical position and not seek to turn the other person's hand but to remain in a neutral position whilst gripping. Deciding the amount of pressure to apply should depend on the person and the specific context and may also be adjusted to equal the pressure that they assert once your hands meet.

- **Deliberate gestures:** Research has shown that people who are confident with their verbal aptitude and who possess a good range of vocabulary will tend to use fewer gestures than others. To give an impression of confidence and to allow our words to possess more meaning it is a good idea to limit the amount of gestures used and to save enthusiastic gesturing for moments when we actually want to convey additional energy or passion.

- **Respect personal space:** Everybody is different and it can be difficult to judge the extent of a person's personal space when we first meet someone. For this reason it is very important to be able to pick up on non-verbal cues about what is appropriate for each individual person and situation. If you notice that someone moves away from you after you have moved towards them, it is a good indication that you have intruded into their personal space and they require a bit more distance. Equally if the person moves towards you it might be a sign that they are feeling a bit distant or disconnected from you and you might want to consider reaching out into their personal space in some way to bring you and the conversation into closer proximity.

- **Make a calm exit:** As the meeting comes to an end it is a good idea to make small preparations so that we exit in a cool and collected fashion. After all that hard work to make a positive first impression it would be a shame to ruin it by leaving on a bad note, so take a moment to check your exit route, to calmly gather your personal belongings and to take a moment to look back and smile as you leave.

Body language is often used in power plays and can be pivotal in deciding the balance of power and influence in social interactions. Certain environmental factors such as furniture and seating arrangements commonly swing the favor one way or the other. If we are aware of these tactics we can avoid being put at a disadvantage by such types of power play. We may also choose use these tactics to our advantage and perhaps create a more equal footing for negotiations or other important interactions to take place.

The furniture designated to each person in an interaction can have a surprising effect on how powerful or powerless they feel in any given situation. We will often notice that people in a position of power or superiority, for example doctors, bank managers or company executives, will have a large comfortable chair that they occupy whilst the other chairs for visitors are much smaller and less impressive. Whilst this may be at least partly because they require a more substantial chair so that they can comfortably carry out their work, it also carries a subtlc message of their superiority and position and that this is their territory where they are 'king'.

How near or far away the people are seated from each other can also be an element that determines the relative power relationship. By placing the chair for your 'visitor' further away you are taking a dominant approach to the meeting. Another way of exerting power over the 'visitor' is to place their chair so that you are facing them directly. If you find yourself in the role of the visitor and you wish to adjust the power play being used against you it is usually possible to subtly move your chair slightly forward or so that it is at a slight angle to the other person. Ensure you make these adjustments as you first come into contact with the chair and move to sit down, as it is more obvious to alter the chair's position once you are already seated.

Conversely, if you find yourself in a position of power and you wish to make your visitor feel more at ease and enter into the conversation on a more equal basis there are certain modifications to the environment that can help you to achieve this. Sit at a slight angle to the person in order to avoid creating any feelings of confrontation. Where possible remove any large or substantial items such as a solid desk that may divide the space between you. Use relaxed, open body language and mirror some of their gestures when appropriate.

# Chapter 8

## Let's be honest: Detecting lies and keeping secrets

One of the most common reasons that people begin to become interested in understanding the intricacies of body language is to be able to tell whether someone is being truthful. Often we will experience the distinct feeling that something doesn't quite add up but we are unable to 'put our finger' on why we our suspicions have been aroused. When we begin to uncover the secrets of body language we are more likely to understand the causes for such hunches and the seemingly indescribable discrepancies that we might sub-consciously pick up on during our interactions with others.

Surprisingly, most people can't tell the difference between a genuine smile and a false smile. The reason for this is that in the instance we are happy that the other person is smiling at us at all and we will automatically respond with a smile irrespective of how honest their initial smile was. We become much more effective at detecting a dishonest smile when we are familiar with the person in question or if we already have some other reason to doubt their sincerity. There are however some general differences that we can learn to recognize in order to determine whether or not those pearly white teeth are actually hiding lies and secrets.

- **Symmetry:** Genuine smiles expand equally across both sides of the face, whilst a fake smile will be uneven. In liars the smile will be more distinct in the left side of the face due to the conscious effort they are exerting in order to produce the facial expression.

- **Neutrality:** People who are lying will actually smile less than those being honest, as they fear being 'caught out'. They are more likely to maintain a neutral facial expression so as to avoid giving an unconvincing smile that may betray their true feelings.

- **The freeze:** A dishonest smile will tend to appear quicker and last longer than an honest smile. The smile might appear to freeze on the face and won't evolve or adjust in the same way that a genuine smile does. The frozen smile can be a real give away as it is the signal that we are most likely to pick up on subconsciously to give us 'that feeling' that someone is being less than truthful with us.

- **Blank eyes:** An honest smile that is expressing true happiness will engage the whole face, especially the eyes. The eyes will tend to actually narrow slightly, the eyebrows will lower and creases will appear at the sides of the eyes and face. A dishonest smile will usually lack the coinciding 'smiling' eyes and the lack of congruence between the mouth and the eyes may give us a valuable clue that something is not quite right.

- **A tense mouth:** One of the most common fake smiles is the wide, tooth-revealing smile where the person's lips are stretched quite tightly and the mouth seems unusually tense. Take note that only the top row of teeth are displayed in this forced smile, giving us a valuable clue that the person is attempting to conceal the whole truth.

As we learnt earlier in the book, the hands are one of the best ways to judge whether someone is being honest with us. Most people will subconsciously use hand gestures that reveal the palms of their hands when they are telling the truth. Amongst the many reasons that people use closed hand gestures or hide their palms is the fact that they may be hiding something from you. Research shows that it is actually incredibly difficult to convincingly tell a lie whilst showing our palms to the other person as the physical act of opening our hands actually compels us to be more truthful. Of course, with practice and good control over our body language we can learn to lie with our hands open. Only the most successful liars will be able to do this convincingly however, as the open palms gesture must appear congruent to other non-verbal signals such as eye contact and facial expression in order to avoid suspicion.

Here are some other telltale signs that someone may well be lying to you...

- **Look to the eyes:** An inexperienced liar will tend to avoid direct eye contact and instead look briefly at lot of different objects in their surroundings. On the other hand, someone who is skilled in deception will actually hold eye contact for slightly longer than someone who is being truthful, making this signal pretty difficult to detect. The pupils of someone being deceitful will also tend to dilate in response to the stress or concentration needed to lie, but again this is one of the most tricky signals to decipher correctly as the pupils may dilate for a number of other reasons including excitement or attraction.

- **Hand to face gestures:** Unnecessarily touching various parts of our face and upper body is a response to stress and therefore tends to occur when we are being dishonest. We may pull on our ears, rub our nose or scratch our neck in an attempt to dispel some of the nervous energy and soothe the discomfort caused by the untruth.

- **See no evil:** Many people feel ashamed or embarrassed when they lie resulting in body language that conveys these emotions such as subtle touching or covering of the eyes. If we are not trying to conceal something shameful, for example if we are apologizing for a mistake, we might find ourselves using our fingers to partly cover one of our eyes. When lying we will tend to use more subtle gestures such as pressing a fingertip to the corner of our eye.

- **Speak no evil:** Even though the words that form the lie are coming from our mouth our body language may still intervene in an attempt to prevent the untruth from emerging. People who are being less than honest will often touch their hand to their mouth repeatedly or cover their mouth in some way whilst telling a lie. Covering the mouth with the hand whilst speaking is a strong indication that the person's words are without real conviction and should be questioned.

- **Closed body language:** Any form of closed body language is likely to present a negative image and will often be seen in amateur liars. The most common signals are arms held close to the body, legs clenched or locked, crossed arms or legs, and standing with the body twisted away from the audience. Inanimate objects may also be used as a barrier between the deceiver and the deceived in an attempt to conceal the truth and protect the person from any ramifications of their lie being exposed.

The further the part of the body is from our brain, the more difficult it is for us to assert conscious control over the signs and signals that it conveys. For example, it is much easier to fake a smile or disguise trembling hands than it is to quell excited feet. In fact, people who are consciously controlling aspects of their body language in order to hide a secret will actually increase the amount of subconscious movements in the furthest reaches of their body such as the legs and feet. It seems that the suppressed signals 'leak out' through the areas that the person has the least control over. This means that in order to have the best chance of decoding hidden messages and revealing the truth we must observe the whole body including the person's legs and feet.

Signs that someone is concealing something from you can be found in the way that they sit or stand. Legs that are locked, either while seated or standing, can be a good indicator that they the person is trying to contain something and their posture is serving to physically assist them with 'keeping it to themselves'. When the feet are withdrawn or hidden in some way this may be a further signal that the person is making a considerable effort to be secretive or dishonest. The direction that someone's feet point towards can reveal the person's deepest desires or the true focus of their attention. This is a little known secret that only people who understand the subtleties of body language share and so remains an excellent way to decipher hidden or mixed messages.

Hidden bonus page…. Shhhhhhhhhh!!! While this book would never encourage people to be untruthful, in some rare situations it might be necessary to succeed in telling a little lie.

Top tips on how to fake it successfully…

- Don't avoid eye contact or look around too much at other things. Keep your gaze calm and controlled and be aware not to close your eyes or blink excessively.

- Avoid touching your face or using any self-comforting gestures

- Keep your mouth relaxed and remember to smile with your eyes

- Keep your laugh reserved but vocal

- Use open body language

- Relax your hands

- Ensure your legs and feet are neutral, not moving but not locked

- Keep your hands away from the mouth or eye area

Other books and Audio by Publisher

**Hypnotise: The Secret Methods to Hypnosis**

**Mind Control Mastery: Techniques to Crush Your Competition (Play Chess, Not Checkers)**

**Methods of Persuasion: How to Turn a No into a Yes**

**Charisma: How to Captivate People**

**Mind Reading-Unlock the Power of Your Mind to get whatever you want**